Love makes the air light

By the same author
*The Linen Bands* (1961)
*The Small Rain* (1963)

# Love makes the air light

## RAYMOND ROSELIEP

W · W · Norton & Company · Inc ·  New York

ACKNOWLEDGMENTS

"Beholder": copyright © 1965 by *America*.
"Hands," "The Minor Elevation": copyright © 1964 by *The American Ecclesiastical Review*.
"Chaplet for Raymond of Pennafort": reprinted by permission from *Blackfriars* (Cambridge, England).
"When Lutes Be Old": copyright © 1962 by *The Carolina Quarterly*.
"Good Night, Mr. Eliot": copyright © 1965 by *The Catholic World*.
"Epithalamion," "For John Kennedy, Jr.," "Poem in Midsummer": copyright © 1964 by *Charlatan*.
"First Communion," "For Barbara, by Mistletoe," "Note, with Glove," "Platonic Lover," "Red Hair": copyright © 1965 by *Chicago Review*.
"Michael Fox and Applecheek Day": copyright © 1965 by The Christian Century Foundation. Reprinted by permission from *The Christian Century*.
"Chalk Talk," "To a Maiden, To Make Much of Time": copyright © 1961, 1965 by *College English*.
"The Bathers," "Namesake," "Put Out a Lunch for Christmas," "A Summer Night at the Keohens": copyright © 1961, 1964 by *The Commonweal*.
From "A Scale of Haiku": "Autumn," "Convolvulaceae," "Crib Song," "Dialogue," "Equation," "Milkweed," "Neighbor," "Notre Dame,"

for my students

past

present

and to come

# CONTENTS

*Love makes the air light*

# MY FATHER'S TRUNK

The soft grainy light of our attic opened
my father's past a little way. His trunk was
a place where years were shut in him like the leaves
of a book whose title alone he displayed
—I wondered if it was mostly about love,
though other strengths were there pressing a vision
on my landscape. I loved the hunters riding
in coontail caps through the ornamental path
inside the lid—I knew by heart the clipping
how he bagged a timber wolf in some woods near
Farley, Iowa, and I sported the brass
knuckles and dangled the billyclub of his
sheriff days, I aimed the elegant pistol
at spider targets—the topmost color in my
first spectrum was the greenpearl of the handle.
Under the sulphur whiteshirts with hard collars
and their beautiful musty smell and the old
leather smell of razorstrop were keys to locks
I never could open; an oval locket,
sealed tight as a dream, carried I always thought
my mother's image. I tried never to laugh
at the ohio matchbox with the sewing
kit of his bachelor days, and though it was
hard to picture the big fingers threading a
needle, I once saw that hand lift a bluebell
from its tower and twirl it like a sparkler.
The letter in the blue envelope he had
never opened bore a script daintier than

my mother's exquisite flourish, and when I
left the blue flap sealed, ordinary breathing
avowed the silence but did not disturb it.
Stale flower smell on another clipping brushed
me like rain: "a knot of English violets
enhanced the heliotrope gown" his bride wore
at their winter wedding, before "a long tour."
And every solitary honeymoon
to the attic filled my boyhood for a while.

One day I heard the plunk-plunk from our chestnut
tree, the gang all pocketing them for our pipes,
small fry on the block playing stickball, the flash
and thrust of limbs. I sat cross-legged before my
father's trunk and the wilderness of myself.
Signs I found in the tenacious silence of
things: I was the black-footed ferret, juggler,
harlequin: I was a touch on the padded
stairs, a balance of milkweed seed, Picasso
performance. With this strange fine figure of man
I had been playing follow the arrow and
capture the flag. Outside, someone was calling
ollie-ollie-oxen-free, and I was free
as a robin, a sun print on a swimmer,
the detached brownleaf and the unfallen snow.
Slyboots of that giant of my childhood, built
so long of limb and entangled in those dark
lidded privacies, I was equidistant
to 'love that makes the air light.' Chip of his strength.

## MAY SONG

Run me, love me
thru the spring hills
and shooting stars
at our ankles.

Love a gray bird
bathing in dust,
laugh your blue
woven wrist.

Tip the bees
to music in
your marrow bone
and mine, and mine.

## LATE SONG

Wake from the burnt grass
when birds sing up and down
and your grass green eyes
fly us home

where light is a crack
on the kitchen floor
and our feet are bare
by the moon-faced clock.

## LOVE SONG

The
      gentian
           sleeps
                in
                    waters
                          that
                              are
                                  your
                                      eyes.

## ENGLISH  SONNET

Put your hand in my hand
and I love you
deeper than Triton's horn
or whorling grotto.

Travel the way
of the vein
with its sea-
dark wine,

quitting the shore
and perishable
turn of your
mortal shell.

Inhabit
my sea going spirit.

## ITALIAN SONNET

When your arms ring my waist
in their tendril
manner, casting a spell
of dark fruit
and rain damp flesh,
keener than sickle
cut or grapefall
on a dry faith:

Then I become aware
and a running vein
in the live
old wineskin
of my self and your
approaching love.

## RED HAIR

Drop your red hair
over my quiet
hand, my arm.
On my breast show it

whatever you find
near a lover's blood,
a man's
terrible wait.

Strand upon strand
let it rest
in its own
desirable light.

Fire
comes together.

## KITCHEN ENTRANCE

you brought these concord
grapes in
from the rain
and draped them
over the side of a milky dish
for the eye to possess
and no other reason

except you forgot
to dry the delicate
doe prints on
the green linoleum

## TO HIS DARK LADY

Intricate on the rock
wall outside my storm
window, that pattern of smoke
flows a shadow like a gown.

I watch snow frame
unheard
the 4/4 time
of an accurate bird.

Flake upon flake,
and sometimes a lull,
make falling dark
interminable.

My world without you, lady,
is white and black and gray.

# THREE NOTES TO TOKYO

*These Chopsticks*

you have sent are one
gift I hold less gingerly
than your giving hand.

.

*Slanted Eyes*

disentangle you
entirely, and I haven't
who am so wide eyed.

.

*Your Rice Fields*

ply their needle point
far from the winter craft in
my picture window.

## ON THE BEHEADING
## OF A BLUE HERON

With the ax of an elbow
you have cut down this heron
from the formal dry wading
over books he was used to,

and in a room now quiet
as some favorite title,
the sprinkle of ceramic,
I die a little.

Slender and nominal friend
he was the souvenir of
another (more final) hand,
or a last holding of love.

Unwittingly you brought down
his silence upon my pride,
definite as rising seed
under the soil of no sun.

Last night I dreamed in color:
I beheld a blue clatter
when you breathed near my shoulder
with his head on a platter.

## PLATONIC LOVER

Though I never rest my hand
on the goldsun of your flesh,
I drain desire from my wish
only when I have wakened;
then I name you plainly friend,
make it clear that my eyes' touch
on your bright mouth is no breach
of the promises I made.

My business runs to handle
affection for its own sake,
and here is my gift of gray:
this matter of icicle
honeycomb, mind you, is like
the certain, erupting day.

## INVITATION TO A
## PROMONTORY
## OVER THE MISSISSIPPI

Sun is a lion
sleek burning,

lucky
bright white stork,

wet buttercup
patch,

chariot
accelerated by a son,

Apollo's
match,

existential
trinket swung,

mind over-
flown.

Each one
is different,

love,
come.

## BEHOLDER

This blue beachflower
nerves a yellow
eye the size of a sand
grain,
I can count five
petals because I am eying it
a finger
away
lying on the island of
no plan.
Up the hairline stem
an insect climbs,
and I track
the spun glass wings
magnifying a
blue significance.
If I hadn't lain here sunning
my innocent back,
the happening would have been
wasted
as last night's dream of two.

# THREE SONGS OF LIGHT

### 1

Beauty is twice
when shared I said
that day & whirled
about to trace
light up a reed
gold as the girl.

### 2

After poured buckets of silence
you open landscape Cézanne
called his playing card, summer pine-
heavy and sky-, dark Provence

mountainfall, roof & sea spilling
blue red brown purple riot
in the eye and hurting a man's
skin when you withdraw, all light.

### 3

A rainbow arc
found the clam's half
burying shell
I gently kick!
And here's my self
only to tell.

# ROOM

across the room
you sit
plain as poem
without image

you touch only
breath
on common
air we are taking

soon you will go
and I will go on
sitting in the room
with possession

## WHEN LUTES BE OLD

I love you
          and kiss you with my mind.
Darling,
      slip into sanctuary
where another angel
            can not tread:

Lie down
      on the moss rug
            again.
               Die.

## POEM IN MIDSUMMER

The bee is drinking at red
clover fountain
more sparkling than
my burgundy blood.

Host of narcissus
breaking over a green
vested body shatters
my day shine.

Darling, this sleight
of hand can wreck our love.
What I speak of
is a single light.

## FOR BARBARA,
## BY MISTLETOE

The taste
of your
holly berry lips
sets a fire-
work off
in an old
hive
of my head.

For all your seven
christmases,
I am given
to your lit eyes
that trust
my trust.

## NOTE, WITH GLOVE

The glove you dropped
(unwittingly) by my single bed
on our christmas eve visit,
with your attending father,

I am returning,
Barbara,
as a lost jewel
or summer rabbit

—I can read
the moonstone and
snowdrop
in its furry text—

and hope
you will be more careful
of a possession
so personal

in the future—I
am alerting your
father protective
as a cedar

roof over a nest,
and here is your glove,
child. Love
later, not yet.

# THE SINGING LESSON

You ask me to sit patient
by your unsinging goldfinch
while you play a record of
a highly inflected meadow.

And I watch your own birdlike
movements, back and forth to the cage,
never more the very child
and woman I love in you,

young Barbara, and a lost
gold summer. In your festival
of field and note I can hear
your voice suddenly high over

the others, even the wakened
throat behind the bars you have
gently tended. Oh your song
sends me out of doors leaping

across your father's prize dahlia
where honeybees wheel in their
nervous dance, and I plunge into
the troubled waters of my being.

# FIRST COMMUNION

The other day
I took my pen-
knife, Barbara,
opened

a door of violet,
was careful
when I felt
the petal

lantern
my touch
(like your unburnt
flesh),

and made this song
for your Communion.

## FOR BARBARA, EIGHT

This horned toad sleeps in your hand
peaceful with all his briar
garmenting, and your fingers
caress him like a flower.

He is attached to the cell
you arrange for his comfort,
shifting ever so slightly
under your browneyed vigil.

You are the fearless jailer
of my growing child day fear
that I should never revel
in the adventure of thorn.

# A SCALE OF HAIKU

RED

A red balloon is
Debora attached to the
red string of my heart.

THRESHOLD

'Love laughs at locksmiths'
but my foot wears out your door-
step, no body comes.

AFTERNOON WALK

I look back to see
the figure I lightly brushed,
now veiled in black rain.

VISITOR, FIRESIDE

Only your eyes hold
the shape of a man's dry love.
Outside, my elms rain.

DIALOGUE

She said "Goodbye." "Goodbye" I said, and my love died.
"Love won't die" she said.


POINT

I'm not your father,
take your head from my shoulder,
my sandpaper face.


PRIEST, EXPLAINING HIS DÉCOR

I picked gray hoping
that visitor who never
should have stayed wouldn't.


PRIEST, TO INQUIRER

This cassock whips my
legs through the four seasons so
I'll know who I am.

## FEUD

That franciscan wren
makes certain scratches across
dominican snow.


## NUN

No lilystick, she
lets her veil to the wind, knows
God best as a gale.


## CONVOLVULACEAE

Morning glories close
their umbrellas, butterfly
rides done for the day.


## MILKWEED

I came just in time:
a whisper later I would
have missed the take-off.

## AUTUMN

Sepia field mouse
and yellow jacket lag by
asparagus fern.


## EQUATION

Boys blow thru the shells
of their plum stones: the air limbs
note on note of birds.


## FAULKNER

A bird sang three bars
meaningless and profound and
a man turned and fled.


## ELEGY: E.E.

cummings left )a leaf)
no lonelier than our (fresh(
fall of labor day

NOTRE DAME

A boy on his knees
by the Virgin's grotto feels
snowfall and a crow.


CHALK TALK

The youth at the black-
board drew a spiral of love,
got on, and it sprung.


SOPHOMORE

For a fifth time Lear
calls *Never* and time is a
bottled fly that drones.


SILL

Collegiate robin
in orange vest, ho, and where
have my students gone?

NEIGHBOR

Hogan's back yard had
a beanflower the color
of our margarine.


NAMESAKE

Wake the sleepy owl.
Our willow buds are just breaking. Little mirror.


CRIB SONG

Close your eyes and ride
my finger, close your eyes and
rock the breaking bough.


FOR CHARLES THOMAS,
ON HIS CHRISTENING

Red are the poppy's
hands and his heart is dark, child,
sleep my poppy song.

## THRENODY

Nephew, go and catch
the crew-cut squirrel who has
gone the way of snow.


## WAKE

The roses I left
in your teacup, mother, grow
purple as my mouth.

## AN ARS POETICA FOR
## JEANNE LOUISE McHALE
## MAKING POEMS
## IN HER ELEVENTH YEAR

That bird deals
in matter
of transubstantial
grain and water.

On the summit
of his show
he lights
a law for you:

his wide
and singing gift
is made
from depth.

A poem
is borne.

# THE ART OF LIGHT

'A POEM . . . SHOULD BE'

Lift this rock and watch
how the bugs run in terror
when the light hits them.


THE HUNTERS

Mallards lie low
when we walk
off with their blue-
green watersilk.


THE CRAFT SO LONG

"Poemman, what hurts?"
"I must find the man I am
in the child I was."


CONTEMPORARY

He pulls his pocket
out to show them
how the dark went
in his poem.

# MARIANNE MOORE, READING

Peacock
elegant the lady
wore a necklace
mirco-
phone
some body else put on
for her
it was so newfangled
(her hat was more familiar though
because it was her tri-
cornered trade mark).
She started
with an
anecdote about Plato
who said if you never knew
a bird could
fly
and discovered your first one
in the grass
you'd know then
that it could.
She intoned
her poems
casually as a summer
afternoon
and in your
scan-
ty

plot
you had the feel-
ing she was fanning dark
jewels at you.
In
the
fall
or lift
of the eyes in
the peacock fan
you couldn't measure
the jewel depth, but you
could recognize a bird to be-
hold and be heard,
one that might
take a par-
ticu-
lar
f
 l
  i
   g
    h
     t

# GOOD NIGHT, MR. ELIOT

*Sweet Thames run softly* run,
the moon exists in spite
of us

From the well of English
you drew a little jug
and shelved it, and shelved it

*Sweet Thames run softly* run,
the moon exists in spite
of us

One infinite distance,
closer to you than us,
closes in, closes in

*Sweet Thames*

# THE WAY OF A BIRD

The eye shut softly,
I lose my students debating
too much reality
after nightingale singing.

Keats, you are obstinate
as a robin
so won't sing
in a cage . . but

There's that thrush again!
—you can't afford
to have him run
you up a pretty bill in *his* store

when you deal at Clementi's.
The way of a poem
is perilous. Rise
and show them.

## GLOSS ON A TEXT
## BY KEATS

Turning full
faced
shadowy
halted:

Ambition, be
air
taken in
dream;

Poetry,
flesh
made
word;

Love, oh mouth
before
space before
mine.

Shadows, go
side faced,
turning,
processional.

# A TUNE FOR MARTY
# IN DARK ADOLESCENCE

make a tune of broken love ah
Iowa bridges fallen down
broken love ah make a tune of
your fair lady

whistle bars a youngman will
dark as falling water
bars awhistle and a youngman
will come tumbling after

put the words down on a stone of
boyhood's growing wall
down the words put on a stone O
Marty humptyfall

# MICHAEL FOX AND APPLECHEEK DAY

*Romeo, come forth; come*
*forth, thou fearful man . . .* III. 3

Michael Fox and applecheek day
take a wintering man outside
where the perfect pitch of a bird
calls his handhold on finity:

so space around Poem, intake,
lookout and ivory tower
diminish with the snow water
or the bell on an icecream cart.

Odd, a man will sigh, how a boy
can close your road to Verona,
stunning the map of Iowa
with light louder than the moon's cry.

Michael Fox and applecheek day
by that girl in the apple scarf
muffle the sound of a dry wasp
and Adam's older offspring. Me.

*(for one of my students)*

# DAVID

You know how fire suppressed burns all the fiercer.
                                    —*Metamorphoses*, IV


He comes to class when he remembers,
and everybody welcomes David
because he's a poet like Ovid
and rakes the adolescent embers,
old fashioned as death. It's wonderful
to be flatbellied and brown from sun,
to have a pitcher's arm, and a hand
gentle for the mulberry petal—
unloaded gravely from a calyx
and folded in Friday's theme On Love
in *Pyramus and Thisbe*. Next week
I'll save my gullible heretics
from David and speak directly of
master Ovid with the tongue in cheek.

# TO A MAIDEN, TO MAKE MUCH OF TIME

Your David fell in & out of love
how-many-spokes-on-a-daisywheel,
but you caught the sand-freckled towel
he threw when he flashed his eye, and dove.

And returned. With linger of mermaid
stirring a breeze with never a gill;
of starfish plunging a starry shell
to prickle the skin of the seaweed.

Girl, lovely as love is flesh & real,
not gone with his wind or falling star,
unwilling to weave any circle
thrice as a charm for your wanderer:
rustling in Julia's leftover silk,
feed David on apple pie & milk.

## CLOWN SONG

Boy of sad
face and dark
head, take
my clown hand

and waggish dog
(here's a hoop
he'll leap
thru), tag

my talkie bird
with a red balloon,
deck a pompon
on this sword

and cut my woe
in two, in two.

## HE WAVED THE GIRL

He waved the girl
off to the
world
out there.

Sat on
a barstool
in
a corner of his soul.

Sipped
the chosen alcohol;
felt
well.

Silence got
more silent.

## GANG

We played harmonicas of redripe melon
on the curb and flung
the rind in the gutter,
all our dime spent.

When bats reeled as bees
under streetlight bloom
we played kick the can,
not wanting to make our 10:30 curfew.

Our dads whistled us in
and we climbed stairs each to his bunk
where death played a trick
on us, our boyhood gone.

# CHAPTER IN ANGELOLOGY

The nun who served religion
in ice cream heaps
to our hungry first grade
dished up angels pink as strawberry,

whip cream light,
genuine as the air
we heard rustle
when those wingmen

winged around our table
tops. Oh we were told
to leave room
on our small red chairs

for the companion spirit
blown to each.
So we sat uncomfortable
on rock of a sister's faith.

This was the year I put away
the things of a child,
too many things
away.

# PUT OUT A LUNCH FOR CHRISTMAS

My brother Louis cut our
fruitcake thicker than a man's
thumb and I poured a water
glass of our father's dark wine.

We slept in the annual
long black stockings of boyhood,
tired below the leaden bell
of a reindeer hurry sled.

We came down in dim morning
to ponder our airy guest,
maybe roll our fingers on
his cake crumbs, breathe from his glass.

A last deceiving Christmas,
we clung to one another,
put out a lunch from practice
with no hope of a father.

# MIRABILIS JALAPA

Who
ever
hung
that
chan-
delier
in
four
o'
clocks
knew
of
light.

## QUIETLY I CAME INTO SPRING

This large dark welcoming to spring
is not exactly what I had expected.
But there he fell:
pitch hooded, royal backed, iridescent barred;
his tail was stiff as a dry broad sail,
he aired nervous spindlelegs on the front lawn,
switching a quick head to eye me
or maybe pin me in his black glance.
When he pecked a tattoo on last year's carob
I could hear my musical top of forty springs ago
make a sound after melody had circled out:
the ticktocking on a brittle clock
or the air when a throat has quit its rattle.

Quietly I came into spring this year:
have not boasted of the arrival,
paid my respects to sap and sun,
seed, egg, bee and dancing foot.
And the purple grackle.

## FARMER, RETIRED

A man under the town clock
on Main Street loiters
before a bucket of lilies
gracing the drugstore entry,
never told they are plastic.

He can smell them: heady as plowed earth
or fluted lettuce a housewife tended
or even pears plunking outside the bedroom.
He is a tintype, still unfooled
so long as bees keep their appointment in his blood.

## TAVERN, TWO SEASONS

### 1

Blown evergreen and red bow
on the snowy air
wave us
laughing to that entrance.

### 2

When silver palm lies on that door
a sleeping hand,
a robin blocks our entry
picking bones of a popcorn box.

# LATE AFTERNOON

*(for David's mother)*

This lady knits
cranberry socks for her
children and
another child come
wandering in
to her african
violet room.
*Mother my feet*
*are dry from*
*walking and their*
*bones are dusky.*
*Measure me*
*in the skeins*
*of your sunfall,*
*in the upper third*
*of your trifocals,*
*burning like snow*
*drops.*

## COUNTRY WALK, WITHOUT MICHAEL

Geese in fluid ticktacktoe
shadow the sky, and their november
horns have roused the morning.

A rusty cornstalk snaps against my
pantleg, whispers indian danger
near the gathered scalp
of this ancient and frosted pumpkin.

I cut routinely thru pampas grass
pearly as a coffin crucifix,

stop to clip some catchweed and berry
branches to cover a pit for
the unsuspecting squirrel,
forward in his red hunter jacket.

I will detain him in the thorn,
as ragged, Michael, as broken water.

## MARKER

In my dream I was a boy
in a coffin and only
my brother came carrying
the sort of gray violet
we picked in Rabbit Hollow
and the shade of his jacket.

My brother is dead tonight
and the woods are blank with snow
and I should never go

# FOR JOHN KENNEDY, JR.

Stand at attention
for a moment
lit as birthday candle
or bullet

This is your father
and our brother
in outer space
weather

Be straight with
your man's
eye on dark
providence

Grow.   You have a flag
and scrap
of black
crepe

# WHEELS

columbine in my brother's tan
fingers whirred
scarlet yellow
spurred

        ✿

cotton candy
spun
in Janet's pink cartwheel
on her lawn

        ✿

Willie's
running
sparkler
spoked our summer

        ✿

a rainbow
leapt
from my musical
top

        ✿

the lion-clipped
airedale
foolishly chased
his lion tail

✿

purple agates
of the Clay Street gang
rolled terror
in our marble ring

✿

above the
bare trees
wind rattled
a rosary of geese

✿

snowman
torso
in the sun
burnt low

✿

over
uneven
earth my father
was darkly driven

# SUMMER NIGHT AT THE KEOHENS

MR.

The chocolate bat
over his bald head rings a
lopsided halo.

MRS.

Gothic arches of
her lupine make me kneel where
I had planned to sleep.

YOUNGEST

Barbara clipped that
tiffany rose to see it
near her sparrow eggs.

KERRY

Red headed girl with
her nose in the firecracker-
rose is too much rose.

KATEY

Her candelabra
fingers glow with the tiny
wicks of the fireflies.


ELDEST

Martha busy in
her kitchen sets a place mat
for a guest not god.

## RIVERMAN

He unfolds the river like a treasure map,
taking the care of a child near a moment
of discovery: and I bury my head
in his explosive sun. The day catches us
and the river frames us beyond our own touch.
His thirty three summers are a stopped hourglass
where my traveling eye burns like thorn. He guides.
We glide into the most secret passages
he has marked from his long boyhood and can share
with a nightcry he must hear under my skull.
The river moves in me as the wild daisy
"big as a button" he had dropped earlier
in my city hand, or as my breathing when
he delayed a water moccasin with his
elm tines, then held it gently at the throat so
I could view the coral tongue and run my knife
lightly against the wonderful saw of teeth.
Under a yellowbirch peeling apricot
and rose and purple, we still the "half a mo-
tor" to fish his boyhood into the man years
and the light he cuts with strength and reverence.
The bluegill on his line stings me with surprise:
it is a cut of jewel in the wet air
and it sings to the dull muskrat and beaver
and the planted deer on fresh run, it whistles
through this hollow driftwood I picked for a lamp,
it jigs before the blue legmaster heron
and thin blackstocking egret. His heavy hand

is one with all splendid space.

                Now the day slopes
and I take my loose leaf notebook ashore, drive
the riverman home in my mind where Simon
Peter once had banked. His name is Louis though,
and he has broken my books like tired nets.

# SHADES OF WHITE

### 1

Cyrano held to
his perfect plume at death time
and even after.

### 2

Henry James counseled
a youth to write loneliness
on his writer's flag.

### 3

A Japanese ran
up to my dead brother's trench
with a pale banner.

### 4

I found something of
you in earth and have loved since
then the daisy seed.

### 5

That one butterfly
pilots a snow covered plane
through the whole summer.

**6**

In my roka blue
cheese glass rue anemones
seem alright for you.

**7**

We shut our eyes by
Dante's God the father where
all color is caught.

# A WASHINGTON TEA, AT 5:00

A tea with Katherine Anne Porter is what
you would expect it to be. Before a long
fifteenth century walnut table cherished
from a monastic refectory, you sit.
Sipping the tallow colored tea with lemon
gold rind twisted like wet embroidery thread.
You mention it is good to be here, letting
the Bach Magnificat in D major claim
your ear as it dims the eye of your hostess
remembering (God knows what man child), and you
take one sugar square more than you wish because
you like to watch the small white fingers plant all
of Ireland's sunlit grass beside your china:
no emerald ever blazed such continent.
You expect that Venetian cherub to slip
down from his votive station of parcel-gilt
bronze, flanking the madonna below a half
length of Christ, and you smile quietly at the
reverent posture, the young genital un-
perturbed in the movement of the August sun.
A sherry tart as crisp as a fall petal,
now some excellent Purcell on gay spinet-
fingering, and the afternoon is an old
man tripping down a gangplank to his own land.
Keeping an eye on the brass foot of Eros
who hauls a dolphin on his shoulders, you wish
for a rapid color change when your hostess
brushes her eggshell gown against their progress,

and that young god blushes in your busy skull.
The lady moves back and forth to her console,
the silver service, your cup, the thronging books:
there is no wilderness of crowds among these
lives, known as true lovers are known. She touches
page and dear page from the lapful she has picked
(once climbing her nephew's perilous little
winding ladder for a Milan leather Keats),
and she reads softly, in English-and-southern
accent, the periods of Henry James, songs
of Breton fishermen, an early cryptic
of Ezra Pound (who declined her offer of
clam broth at St. Elizabeth's), Eudora
Welty opening her Post Office story,
J. F. Powers on the golf links with Father
Urban, a musical paragraph about
oysters by the wife of Robert Penn Warren,
notes from Ovid's Orpheus. When you summon
another Catherine who said "My nature
is fire," the stonewalls of Siena crackle
in the sky of your mind. You drop an index
finger on the walnut heart patch, then you trace
the leaf pattern suggesting the modest fig
those old friars surely slipped over Venus.
Music for the funeral of Queen Mary
puts italics on the clock, so you are careful testing the almond on your teeth, catching
the salt on your tongue like a new baptism:

You are a child before grief and the lady
who has mingled on deck with lovers and fools,
voyaging this late afternoon to deeper
sea, more golden than tea in your bonewhite cups
and her robins outside too tired to quarrel.

## FLANNERY O'CONNOR 1925–1964

Love cuts like cold wind
away from the summer will of God.
There's hardly a discipline for dying.
Insuck of breath,
lemon light.

The wood thrush spends
four formal notes,
a honeybee bungles
the legs' scissoring,
a switch of blackberry bush
catches the passing sleeve.

A 'hundred eyes' stall
the blue-green flesh.

Spark
 breaks
  among stubble.

# THE THIRTEENTH OF NOVEMBER
# NINETEEN HUNDRED AND SIXTY FOUR,
# CHICAGO

*(for Henry Rago)*


Long gowned and black
tied at eight thirty one
invading Orchestra
Hall to hear some poets beat their music,

we are met by one another
and the inevitable
colored boy offering
the dusky shoe a

'quick rub for 6 cents,'
everybody refusing,
none of us wearing enough
common sense

to tell his public
laughter needs just half
a dozen of these gilt
coins to make

him believe in our shows.
Late, we scurry in
to the dim house, *s-s-sh,*
the fiddlers have lifted their bows.

## 'UPON CHERRY-STONES'

### SPRING HOMILY

That blackfriar ant
mounts the pulpit of a hair
to preach from my arm.

### SKYLINE

One sunrise and sun-
set are enough for a May
fly life, even mine.

### CONCERT

Pain is transcendent
when you are listening to
mosquito music.

### HERON

Bungling bird! I thought
I was safe in my tree house.
Your leg pierced my roof.

PRESENCE

God is in the earth, air,
water, the ciborium
of my self, fire.


AFTER A WORDSWORTH SEMINAR

The boy said, "I'm proud
to know Michael, but don't you
tell my old father."


ENROUTE

It's remarkable
how you don't meet somebody
exactly like you.


LOVER

Innocent as ice
cream, his hand on the oval
of your white belly.

NOTICE

Lying barefoot in
my berrypatch, watch for that
foxy Don Russell.


DECLARATION

His words "I love you"
hang from his mouth, caught in their
comic strip balloon.


A DOUBLE BRANDY FOR
DR. JOHNSON, PLEASE

Sir, all's well. Cheers for
the endearing elegance
of female friendship.


FALL

Gouge out the gold leaf
from my retina—I've found
it with my white cane.

HEIGH-HO THE HOLLY

Now that friends are gone,
come to the begging bowl of
my hand, ragged flakes.


MOMENT

I get the feeling
of having been here before,
marblewhite mother.


AFTER LOVING

Wear the poet's mask
saying you'll manage without
her. Be quick. Drink up.


PACT

Let's exchange poems
as Hamlet and Laertes
exchanged forgiveness.

POETS

God is like me, he
makes from nothing, only I
am caught with a script.


DYLAN

If she phones say I'm
out gathering images
and will miss supper.


COMPOSERS

Basho and bitter
cricket play equally well
on my western ear.


THE HAIKU

Granule of being,
Fuji climb: shadow from shade,
star capful, larkhold.

BLOSSOM

One more entrechat,
fluff cherry, before you turn
to flesh, skeleton.

"Milton, Madam, was a genius that could carve a Colossus
from a rock, but could not carve heads upon cherry-stones."
—Dr. Samuel Johnson to Miss Hannah More who had
    expressed a wonder that the poet of *Paradise Lost*
    "should write such poor sonnets."

## SAILBOAT WITH THREE

The painter brushed a blessing
on early light
when sails of calla lilies
rooted his feet.

The priest limned a cross
near a relic fish
toppling lavabo
at Pilate's dish.

The ordinary youth
in blue jeans
let water pour his mouth
incomparable wines.

Under the fiery tongue
of their spinnaker
three lives reached
one another.

## FLEE

I
run
from
me;

puff;

step
out
of
(lord)

foot
step:
soled,
souled,

sold.

## CHAPLET FOR RAYMOND
## OF PENNAFORT

### 1

The plain chronicler
said, as a boy you had an
old man's mind and heart.

### 2

It took a poet
hand to put law and order
in our decretals.

### 3

You heard confessions
doggedly as the camel
driver of Mecca.

### 4

Only a kinsman
touches a poor body so.
Jew. Moslem. Brother.

### 5

A hundred sixty
leagues, some cried, is a big stretch
for a cloak and staff.

## 6

I have a snip of
your bone, light as a sail: where
do I go from here?

## 7

My sea-gone student
named his first boy after you.
Help him sail. Help me.

## LETTER RECEIVED

Dear father, I am gliding away
from intangible loving and more
gently (a lover will guess) than I
had broken the umbilical cord.

When kneeling behind your rubric whirled
over grape in morning bravado,
I am easing away from your cold
espousal and terrible shadow.

Father forgive me, I am drifting
on the new potencies of manhood,
setting alarms that will some time ring
from the surf sound of blood in my side, . . .

headed for other billowing love
than your dark red grail of make believe.

# MY DAY AS HE GOES

*for Daniel: anima naturaliter christiana*


The air is honey
heavier on him and his
softgreen cadillac

than he can collect
without a mirror or my
vantage retina.

Hair blanch as his white-
walls, cockled as a swimmer's,
Lyciad features

october rallied
from vacation tennis court
or shadowless yard

where Aristotle's
children trot to pillage *De
Amicitia,*

he is going: clean-
tired and grasshopper headed
for catacomb years.

I could pray the face
(not at all tight on its scheme
of bone) chill as mine,

though never will him,
Christ, my dead man bones knocking
my day as he goes.

## THE BATHERS

Men will find the Wapsipinicon
waiting on shinbone and knucklebone
and spirit. Men together. Alone.

Once upon an August time three men
went out to grace the water roaming.

One left groping for the skeleton
of the fish and wanted to feel it
again briefly, as the cut of salt
in a daydream of his infant tongue.

The second lolled the way streetboys loll,
took pleasure in the minnow nibbling
his sumptuous hips pleasant to turn
in the rippling, away from his soul.

The last man threw his body across
a thicket of water and he dove
as a lover as reckless in love,
with wilderness flesh to the Christfish.

Three men found the Wapsipinicon:
remembered.  tingling.  and a Jordan.

# HANDS

### 1

Mary of Magdala
pressed
her long hair
on excellent flesh.

### 2

Martha's sister Mary
poured
300 denarii
of nard.

### 3

Judas rang
a bell or
silver
saltcellar.

### 4

The stark young man
without name
reached for dark
to robe shame.

5

When Peter rubbed his palms
by evening fire
a girl
made him aware.


6

Pilate put the weight
of three days in
a small
domestic basin.


7

Heavyweight
**Christ**
beat the night
with fullblown fist.


8

**When his spear**
bit
the core
Longinus pushed it.

## 9

The Virgin
touched her grief
lightly to a man's
sleeve.

# HIGH OVER MAGDALA

Wind touches her
on the lean hill
where she is shaking like a rained on
rose
or can hear her bones dance

death in the hall of flesh
Loosened tangles of her hair
and their curved falls
bring a man's sweet scent
and new dimension to singleness.

Darkness will harden her:
bitten lids of her eyes
drop
properly before linen light
and nondescript gardener.

## NIGHT PIECE

The smooth body of Christ
white as a stripped willow
sleeps above the thin
line of a boy
traced on linen.
Once he tries to send
his hand thru sifted light
up to the darkwine cave:
to give what he does not own,
put his fingers empty
into the side,
know he has given.
But only his cheeks and lips
draw claret
from the night lamp,
and he shivers
the ground of his room.
He is the roaring child, half
wakened under a shaving of
moon like a curl
by his father's plane.
He bargains sleep
to ail graystone
in his mind with the old
dice of dream work:
no bird will flute him home.

# SONG FROM AN ENCLOSURE

They say you are
nearest when
far away.

I would like
to feel you if only
breath on my cheek

or quick
collision
of skin

to bother
belief, elusive-
my-love.

O
room is wide and the world is
wide

Christ!
and it's that way
inside my fortress of flesh.

# THE MINOR ELEVATION

Christ hung heavy in my right
hand etching crosses over
the lake of chalice where he
swam my strongbodied lover.

Through him and with him and in
him is to you God, I said,
peering into the wineness
of wine, the breadness of bread.

A fruitfly cut a zigzag
trail through the hole of my thumb-
tip and joining forefinger
and housekeeper's phlox grown numb.

A cold sparrow sang a cold
song in the imperfect nave,
away from the autumn rain,
less than mildly attentive.

The chilly *mea culpa*
or an earlier playground's
*run sheep run* became only
a frozen breathmark of sound.

The whorling, knotted, jointed
frame that was I delayed, bi-
secting the table of food
and a whole table of sky.

Cartwheel, handspring and leapfrog
are boygames, I kept saying,
and stood heavy soled and caught
at our identifying:

with the altar cross I picked
out from the bluegrape mirror
my face in the pool of Christ:
it shone like an open sore.

## CANTICLE

He is a fountain sealed
with honeysuckle flavor,

sea bed
laboring pearl,

aspergillum
conch of sea sound.

His mouth is odor of apple,
throat of best wine.

His shoulders tremble mountain air,
ocean stirs in his loins.

Run the heels wind
and win him,

as the roe leap to him
before the bright shape of sleep.

# EPITHALAMION

*for Charlotte, at the altar*


A stained
glass pelican
rubrics your white gown
when sun rains.

Your black forest
eyes carry
the sweet male body
light as candlepoint.

His ring is a tongue
of fire
lapping
softer than water.

He shoots up
from Lebanon
on your keen
marble step.

Diamond is
in his navel
and his loins are a topaz
chalice well.

You attend
his wheatfield
silver
on air.

His vineyard
spins
wet rubies for
your hands.

Lily thin
you turn
to his
bee gold touch.

Christ
the
pelican be
your carnival of flesh.

# FOR DENISE, DISTRACTING

Girl sudden
as yellow rainfall
running a yellow

vein thru the birdwing
in my poem,
you are tampering with

artifact and fact:
a bluejay
candled branch

breaks
when you kneel on the gray
marble of my mind.

I will leave confessional
foolscap
littered with birds

to take communion
in the late air
where light is at a premium.

## THE SMOKE SMELL OF SPRING

The smoke smell of spring and your smoky hair
hum in the nostril,
that kid with the red cap fires a hardball
over the sun,
a housewife tinsels the branching clothes line
brighter than her sunburn,
a spider stubs a toe on rock
footlighting a ballet of violets.

In these middle years I hail my stance:
rise, move, turn,
a priest darkgolden,
oiled and wined for the dance.